Contents

Transport

People travel

in every culture.

Let's see how other people

around the world travel.

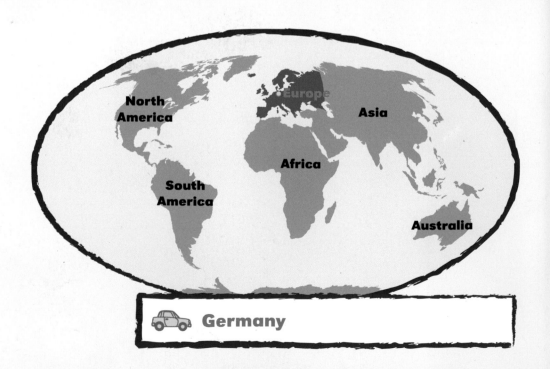

North America

Europe

Asia

Africa

South America

Australia

Germany

Going to school

These girls in China
walk to school.

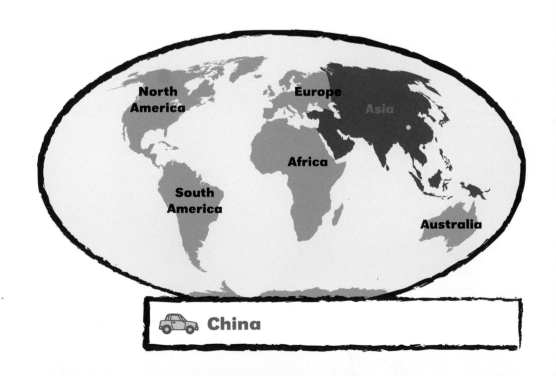

North
America

Europe

Asia

Africa

South
America

Australia

China

These boys in
the United States
go to school by bus.

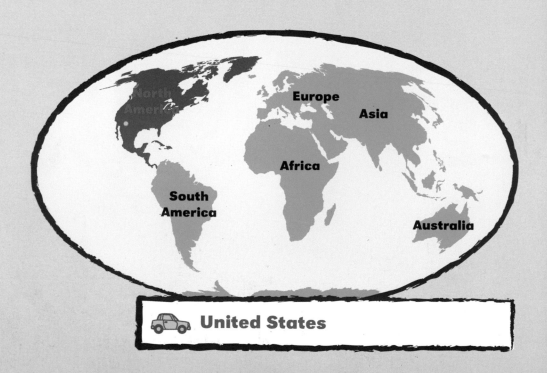

Europe

Asia

North America

Africa

South America

Australia

🚗 United States

These girls in Japan
go to school by train.

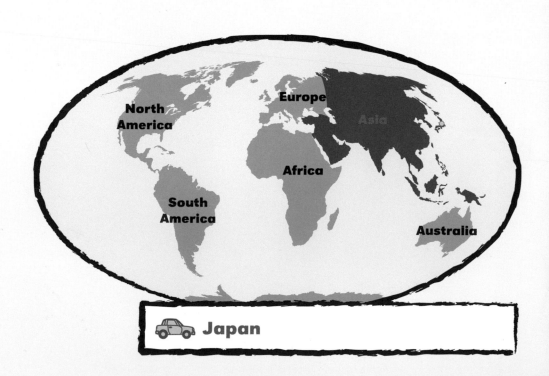

These kids in Cambodia
paddle boats to get
to their floating school.

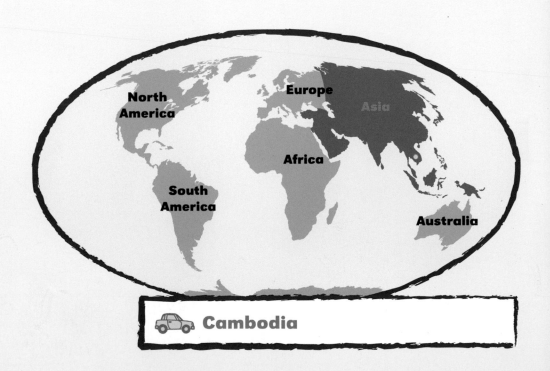

North
America

Europe

Asia

Africa

South
America

Australia

Cambodia

Going to other places

People in Australia

travel by monorail.

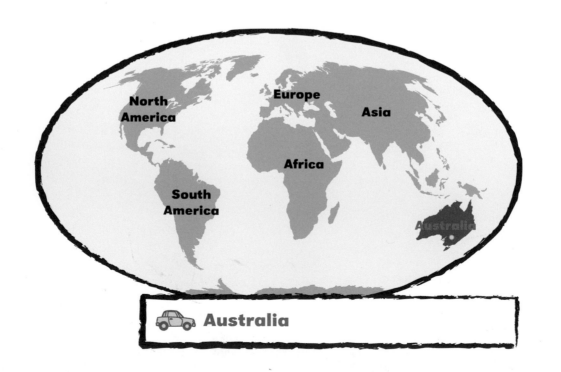

Australia

Travellers in Bolivia
take an aeroplane
to another country.

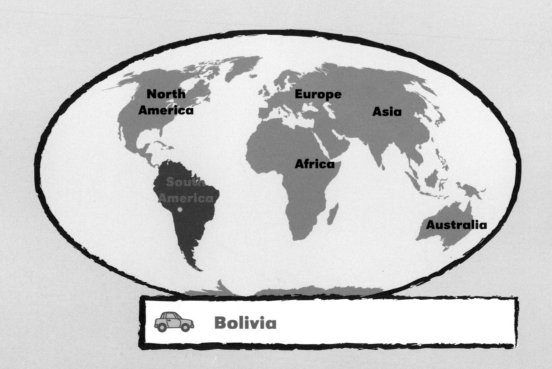

North
America

Europe

Asia

Africa

South
America

Australia

🚗 Bolivia

A boy in Canada

rides a snowmobile.

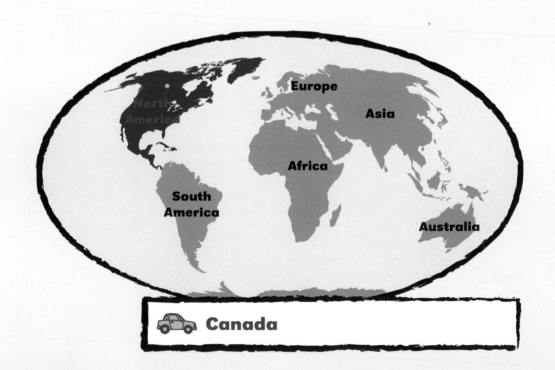

Canada

On the go!

Around the world,

people travel on buses,

bicycles and animals.

How will you travel today?

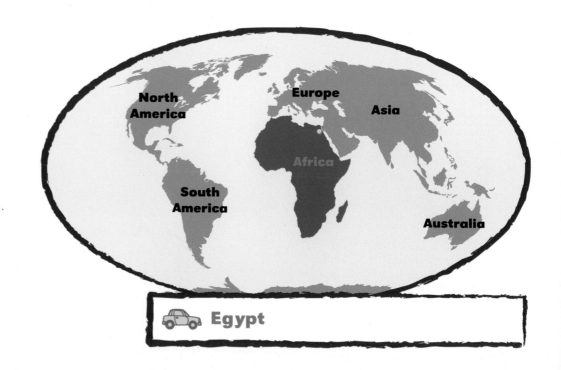

Egypt

Glossary

culture   way of life, ideas, customs and traditions of a group of people

monorail   train that runs on one rail, usually high above the ground

paddle   push through the water with an oar

snowmobile   vehicle with skis used to travel over snow

travel   go from one place to another

Find out more

How We Get Around (My World Your World), Ellen Lawrence (Ruby Tuesday Books, 2015)

My First Book of Transport, Charlotte Guillain (A&C Black, 2012)

Transport Around the World (Children Like Us), Moira Butterfield (Wayland, 2016)

Websites

http://easyscienceforkids.com/all-about-transportation/
Fun facts about different types of transport.

http://www.bbc.co.uk/education/topics/zt2mn39/videos/1
Videos about different methods of transport around the world.

Index